THE
PILL-BOXES OF FLANDERS

By

COLONEL E. G. L. THURLOW, D.S.O., p.s.c.

With a Foreword

By

General Sir Charles Harington, G.C.B., G.B.E., D.S.O., p.s.c., late Major-General General Staff, Second Army, British Expeditionary Force

The Naval & Military Press Ltd

Published by

The Naval & Military Press Ltd
Unit 5 Riverside, Brambleside
Bellbrook Industrial Estate
Uckfield, East Sussex
TN22 1QQ England

Tel: +44 (0)1825 749494

www.naval-military-press.com
www.nmarchive.com

In reprinting in facsimile from the original, any imperfections are inevitably reproduced and the quality may fall short of modern type and cartographic standards.

FOUND IN A PILL-BOX AT PASSCHENDAELE ON ITS RE-OCCUPATION

1. *"This position will be held and the section will remain here until relieved*

2. *The enemy cannot be allowed to interfere with this position*

3. *If the section cannot remain here alive, it will remain here dead, but in any case it will remain here*

4. *Should any man through shell-shock or any cause attempt to surrender, he will remain here dead*

5. *Should all guns be blown up, the section will use Mills grenades and other novelties*

6. *Finally, the position will be held as stated"*

THE AUSTRALIAN MACHINE-GUNNERS, WHO HAD OCCUPIED THE POSITION, LAY AROUND—DEAD.

[*From the Library at Talbot House, Poperinghe.*

CONTENTS

		Page
FOREWORD	... ...	7
CHAPTER I.	Introductory	9
CHAPTER II.	Notes on the construction of the German concrete shelters and emplacements	11
CHAPTER III.	How to reach the pill-boxes	13
CHAPTER IV.	Essex Farm and Hussar Farm, Potijze	15
CHAPTER V.	St. Julien, Wieltje, Kitchener's Wood, Pilckem ...	17
CHAPTER VI.	Borry Farm, Frezenberg, Fitzclarence Farm ...	27
CHAPTER VII.	The Area between the Ypres-Menin Road and the Ypres-Lille Road	28
CHAPTER VIII.	Wytschaete-Messines Area	31
CHAPTER IX.	1918. The withdrawal in the Salient and the final advance	37
ENVOI	... ...	39
APPENDIX, Key to Cemeteries shewn on Map		40
INDEX	... ...	44

ILLUSTRATIONS AND SKETCHES.

Sketch A showing position of pill-boxes near St. Julien and Triangle Farm	Page 16
German Concrete Blockhouse at Alberta	Facing page 22
Old British Observation Post, Hussar Farm, Potijze ...	Facing page 23
Air Photographs showing ground north-west of Frezenberg before and after bombardment, 1917	Facing page 26
British dugouts at Lankhof Château	Facing page 27
Sketch B showing position of pill-boxes in the vicinity of Pilckem	Page 30

FOREWORD

By the efforts of Toc H and the British Legion some 180 of the old original pill-boxes in the Ypres Salient have, with the concurrence of the Belgian Government, been preserved for the younger generation to realize what they meant to their elder brethren.

Those who have seen them in war can only wish to forget them—strongholds for one moment, death traps the next. How well I remember the morning after our capture of the Messines Ridge! I crawled into a German pill-box only to find four German Officers sitting round a table as if they had been playing Bridge—all sitting up but stone dead without a mark on them. They had all died from the shock of the explosion of our mines under the Messines Ridge. It was a pill-box quite near the great Spanbroekmolen Crater.

To the younger generation I would say, these things happened. You owe your liberty to the glorious fellows who fought in these places and held the Ypres Salient against terrific odds. They gave their all that those who came after them might never see the like again. We can never betray that trust. When you visit these pill-boxes in the Ypres Salient, think of those men who lie there. They died for us. What glorious unselfishness and self-sacrifice! Are we to-day playing square by them? Surely we cannot break that great trust!

At the time you visit these pill-boxes you will visit our Cemeteries in the Ypres Salient. Your thoughts will turn from the awfulness of those pill-boxes to the peace and beauty of those Cemeteries—to those gallant lads of our great Empire who lie there. You will be justly proud of them. You will also be proud that their names and graves are preserved as you will see them with such quiet beauty and dignity. You will see some of that great and unselfish body of men who, under the Imperial War Graves Commission, look after those graves. Hours of work mean nothing to them. They tend those graves just as if in each one a son of theirs was buried. We owe much to those men.

And, lastly, on your tour you will visit the Menin Gate. You will stand there and see the names inscribed on those memorial tablets. You will stand there and hear the Belgian buglers sound the " Last Post " on bugles presented by the British Legion. This is done by our Belgian Allies every night. I was present with my late Chief — Field-Marshal Lord Plumer of Messines — the defender of the Ypres Salient—when he unveiled the Menin Gate Memorial. No one who was present will ever forget his tribute to the glorious men of the Second Army who, under his command, held the Ypres Salient against terrific odds. His words " They are not gone from us, they are here," will never be forgotten by anyone who heard them.

                C. H. HARINGTON, General,

                    late M.-G. G.S., Second Army.

ALDERSHOT,
    28th December, 1932.

THE PILL-BOXES OF FLANDERS

CHAPTER I.
INTRODUCTORY.

This brief sketch does not profess to be a history of any kind, nor does it aspire to any literary merit. It has been compiled with the object of providing for pilgrims and others a short account of the more important events connected with certain of the concrete blockhouses and shelters (nicknamed "pill-boxes" by the British soldier), which, thanks to the efforts of Toc H and the British Legion, now remain in the vicinity of Ypres.

These pill-boxes are the chief reminders of the scenes of heroic deeds, of comradeship, and of the prowess of those who fought in "the Salient" during the memorable years of 1914-18. They are relics which will enable the younger and coming generations to visualise something of the great spirit of sacrifice shown by their elder brethren during the four years which covered possibly the fiercest fighting and certainly the worst conditions of warfare that the world has ever known. The British attacks in the Ypres Salient were delivered from shell holes, from water-logged and demolished trenches, over ground which was in many cases nothing less than a veritable quagmire, against perfectly sited and admirably constructed defences manned by soldiers whose fighting qualities have never been in doubt.

The identification of the various concrete blockhouses and shelters, which now remain, has not been by any means an easy task, for during the battles of 1917, as a result of the terrible weather and the incessant shellfire, the whole terrain became completely obliterated. Ordinary landmarks disappeared, streams ceased to exist, woods were effaced and many of the roads vanished. Consequently, the individual officer or man was often unable to fix with any degree of accuracy his position or that of his unit in the advance. All that remained were the innumerable pill-boxes, the existence of which was, in very many cases, quite unexpected.

Fortunately, however, some of the Divisional and Regimental histories furnish certain clues by means of which, as well as by a close study of the G.H.Q. trench maps and of the line of advance of each unit concerned, it has been possible to piece together the story of these pill-boxes.

THE PILL-BOXES OF FLANDERS

The origin of the nomenclature of places in the Ypres neighbourhood is interesting. Practically all the farm names shown on the present British maps were bestowed during and after the battles of April-May, 1915, and were not on the early maps. Previously, localities had been described by means of map squares. On the Belgian maps most of the farms were unnamed and, indeed, had no names. All that the inhabitants admit is that a farm was identified by its owner's name, or the name of some former owner. Thus, " Mousetrap Farm," marked merely " Château " on the Belgian map, was known to the Belgians and French as " Château du Nord," to the Germans as " Wieltje Château," and to the majority of the British as " Shell Trap Farm." Later it was changed by Corps Orders to " Mousetrap Farm." Not all the farms have been rebuilt on exactly the same sites they occupied in 1914. In most cases they are nearer the main roads. The villages are all small except Langemarck, Boesinghe, and Messines. St. Julien, Wieltje, Frezenberg were classed as " hameaux." St. Julien, for instance, in 1914 had only 190 houses, including outlying farms, and 950 inhabitants.

The compiler of these notes desires to tender his most grateful thanks to the Curator and Staff of the Imperial War Museum, to the Staff of the Historical Section of the Committee of Imperial Defence, to the Ypres League, to Toc H, to the Editor of the " Emblem," to Hon. Lieutenant M. de Hasque, Belgian Army, and to Lieut.-General Salzenberg, late Commander of the Pioneers of the German 15th Army Corps, who so kindly assisted in supplying the information contained therein ; also to Colonel E. C. Heath, D.S.O., General Secretary, British Legion, to Captain Cyril Falls and Mr. E. A. Dixon, Historical Section, Committee of Imperial Defence, to Captain G. E. De Trafford, M.C., Secretary of the Ypres League, to Mr. L. P. Yates Smith, and to Colonel M. Earle, C.B., C.M.G., D.S.O., whose helpful criticisms have been of the utmost value ; lastly to M. Molitor, D.C.M., who has translated this work into French.

The Appendix, which contains the Key to the Cemeteries shown on the 1/40,000 Map, has been reproduced by kind permission of the Ypres League.

THE PILL-BOXES OF FLANDERS

CHAPTER II.
NOTES ON THE CONSTRUCTION OF THE GERMAN CONCRETE SHELTERS AND EMPLACEMENTS.

The construction of the German concrete shelters and emplacements (Mannschafts - Eisenbeton - Unterstände or " Mebu " for short) was commenced in the Ypres area early in 1915 and was continued without interruption up to the commencement of the Battles of Ypres, 1917. The original idea of these concrete shelters was to provide protection for supports and reserves against the continuous fire of field guns and against individual shells from 15 c.m. field howitzers. These were followed by the solidly constructed blockhouses and machine-gun emplacements which proved such effective centres of resistance. The building of these structures was carried out by Fortress Engineers and Pioneers and also by Civil Engineers with previous peace-time experience in the construction of concrete work.

Ferro-concrete was used from the very first in preference to plain concrete, but to begin with the reinforcement was not entirely satisfactory, as steel joists, screw pickets and any kind of scrap-iron were thrown in and buried in the concrete. Later, this form of construction gave place to $\frac{5}{8}$-inch round iron rods uniformly distributed over the whole structure, as it was found that the vibrations in girders, rails, screw pickets, etc., had a more disturbing effect on the mass of concrete than the vibrations in the rods. The front walls and roofs of the shelters were from $2\frac{1}{2}$ to 3 feet thick, and the surrounding earth was heaped up to a thickness of from 7 to 15 feet.

At the start, sand and road material for the manufacture of the concrete was requisitioned locally, but later the gravel for the best quality concrete was brought from the Rhine through Holland *via* the Meuse and Scheldt in barges and by rail. It consisted of water-worn gravel, of flintstone and quartz broken to about $\frac{1}{2}$-inch gauge. The sand was mostly coarse, sharp and clean. The best concrete shelters were quite capable of resisting direct hits by six-inch howitzers, heavy trench mortars and artillery of even greater calibre. In fact, in many cases the effect of shellfire on these structures was practically nil. As an instance, it is worth recording that a concrete work constructed inside the buildings of a

THE PILL-BOXES OF FLANDERS

farm was bombarded by both sides for over a month and was none the worse. In another case a large shell landed on the ground close to one wall and the blockhouse simply settled down in the shell hole without being in any way damaged.

The small single chamber dug-outs as, for instance, those at St. Julien in the old Canopus Trench and at Wieltje in the Cambrai and Call Trenches, were sited inside the actual trenches with the upper parts protruding just above ground level. The machine-gunners were kept under shelter till required and then came up and fired their weapons over the parapet. The roofs of the dug-outs were covered with about 18 inches of earth, which had the effect of camouflaging them completely. Pockets for grenades were inserted about one foot below the top of the shelter by hollowing out a space in the concrete.

Machine-gun emplacements were frequently hidden inside houses or located in brick structures designed to imitate houses. The small fort or blockhouse was another type of " Mebu." It stood well above ground level with loopholes and slits for riflemen and machine gunners and, in some cases (*e.g.*, at Alberta), with an emplacement on the top. To capture defence works of this nature was obviously a task of the utmost difficulty, though it is an undeniable fact that there were many cases of individual men crawling up and actually putting the garrison out of action by dropping a bomb into the interior through one of the firing slits.

It can be realised, therefore, that the German High Command insisted on the provision of the best possible protection for their men. On the British side some idea seems to have been current that such works were not worth the labour or the cost, but probably the real reason was the fear that a lack of the offensive spirit might have been engendered if the troops had been provided with such solid defences.

CHAPTER III.

HOW TO REACH THE PILL-BOXES.

In order to reach the different groups of pill-boxes the following itineraries are suggested. In every case it is assumed that the pilgrim starts from the town of Ypres.

Essex Farm.   A I.

Leave by the Rue de Dixmude and follow the Dixmude–Ostend Road. These dug-outs are in the canal bank close to Essex Farm Cemetery and about 1½ miles from Ypres.

Pilckem.   B I.

Leave by the Rue de Dixmude, bear right, and at the crossroads about 500 yards farther on turn left (straight on to St. Jean and Wieltje). Two miles from this point the road forks—that on the right leads to Minty Farm Cemetery, just beyond which are the dug-outs and blockhouses at Macdonald's Wood and Grune Farm (B I, 6, 7, 8, 9, 10).

The left-hand road passes Gournier Farm (B I. 3), and the site of Canister Trench (B I, 4, 5). About 1,000 yards from Gournier Farm a rough track on the left leads to the pill-boxes at Iron Cross.

By following the track past Grune Farm, it is only a short distance to Kitchener's Wood and the group of works round St. Julien (A II).

Wieltje, St. Julien.   A II., A III
                                              B II., B III

Leave by the Rue de Dixmude, bear right and keep straight on for St. Jean. At Wieltje the right-hand fork leads to the blockhouses and dug-outs at A III. These commence 350 yards beyond the village and on both sides of the road. About 1½ miles farther along this road Pond Farm (B III. 1, 2) is reached.

The left-hand fork at Wieltje (the main road to Poelcapelle and Bruges) leads to the works at A II. and B II.

The line of shelters A II. 2–59, is just about one mile from Wieltje. Full details are given in Chapter V. as to the best method of visiting this group. About ¾ mile north of

THE PILL-BOXES OF FLANDERS

St. Julien is Vancouver cross-roads, B II. (Triangle Farm and the Maison du Hibou) being on the left.

Leave by the Menin Gate and take the Zonnebeke Road. To reach Hussar Farm (B VII.) take the turning to the right in Potijze. Continue by the main road to Frezenberg. The pill-boxes south of Borry Farm are on the left of the road about 650 yards east of Frezenberg.
<small>B VII. and B IV.</small>

Leave by the Menin Gate and take the Menin Road; $\frac{3}{4}$ mile beyond Hooge take the left-hand fork and after about 100 yards keep straight up a rough track. This leads to Glencorse Wood and Fitzclarence Farm (B V.).

To reach the Sanctuary Wood dug-outs (A IV.) continue along the Menin Road to "Clapham Junction" (about 300 yards from the fork referred to above) and take the by-road to the right.
<small>A IV., B V., A VIII.</small>

The German Headquarter Shelter at Gheluvelt (A VIII.) is about 250 yards beyond the cross-roads in the village and on the south side of the road.

A V. **Bedford House and Lankhof Farm.**

Leave by the Lille Gate. Bedford House is $1\frac{1}{2}$ miles along this road on the left; Lankhof Farm being about 500 yards beyond the Château on the same side.

A VI. **Messines, Wytschaete, Spanbroekmolen (or Lone Tree) Crater.**

Leave by the Lille Gate. Take the right-hand fork at St. Eloi. This leads direct to Wytschaete and Messines.

To reach the Spanbroekmolen (or Lone Tree) Crater, bear right in Wytschaete and follow the Kemmel Road. Take the second turning to the left (about $1\frac{1}{4}$ miles from Wytschaete Village). About $\frac{1}{2}$ mile down this road on the left-hand side the crater will be found immediately opposite Lone Tree Cemetery. Lumm Farm (A VI. 9) is about halfway between Wytschaete and Messines and 200 yards off the road on the east side and north of the London Scottish Memorial.

B VI. **Oosttaverne, Deconinck Farm, etc.**

Leave by the Lille Gate and take the left-hand fork at St. Eloi (main road to Lille). The various pill-boxes in this group are close to this road between St. Eloi and Gapaard.

CHAPTER IV.

ESSEX FARM; HUSSAR FARM, POTIJZE.

Essex Farm. A I. 1

The concrete dug-outs alongside the main Ypres–Boesinghe road at Essex Farm, just north of the Cemetery, were used as a dressing station from 1915 to about August, 1917. Many casualties from the 51st (Highland) Division and also from the 38th (Welsh) Division were dealt with here during the Battles of Ypres, 1917.

Hussar Farm, Potijze. B VII.

A British observation post constructed inside the original farm buildings. It escaped destruction despite four years of enemy bombardment.

THE PILL-BOXES OF FLANDERS

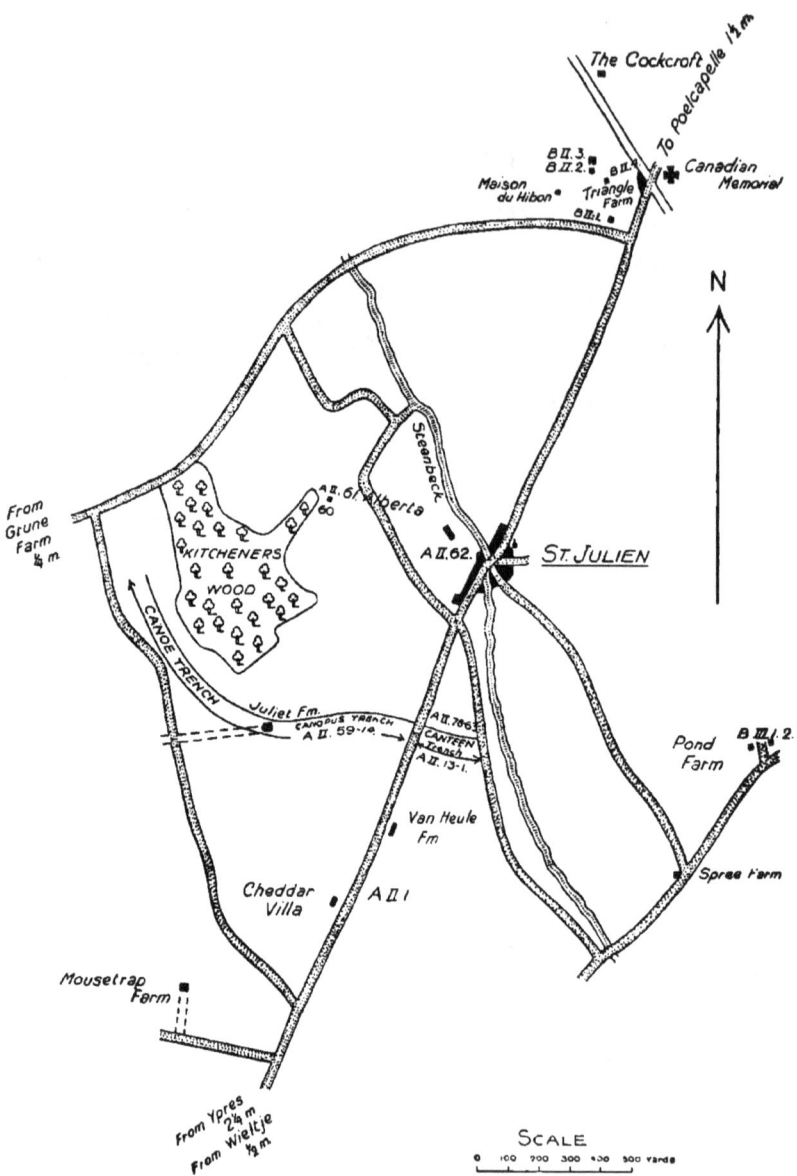

SKETCH A—Showing position of Pill-boxes near St. Julien
(For continuation westward see Sketch B)

THE PILL-BOXES OF FLANDERS

CHAPTER V.

ST. JULIEN, WIELTJE AND THE BLOCKHOUSES BETWEEN KITCHENER WOOD AND PILCKEM.

These are grouped under the headings A II., A III., B I., B II., B III. on the map.

In order to get some idea of this interesting area it is advisable to make for the point where the line of concrete structures is astride the Ypres-Poelcapelle Road, about a mile from Wieltje and some 600 yards south of the Church in St. Julien. There, stand on top of the nearest pill-box on the west side of the road and face towards Ypres. This is the site of the defensive system which was known by our troops as Canteen, Canopus and Canoe Trenches (A II. 2–59 and 63–76 on map). Canteen Trench (A II. 2–13 and 63–76) was on the east of the road, Canopus and Canoe (A II. 14–59) on the west. Canoe Trench ran from just north of Juliet Farm, which is about 500 yards to the north-west of your present position, thence along the west side of Kitchener's Wood. The trees of this wood can be clearly seen just to the north of Juliet Farm. The dug-outs and concrete emplacements which now exist were actually in those trenches and formed part of the German second line defensive system. To the north can be seen two rather isolated but distinctive blockhouses standing well above ground level. These are the redoubtable Alberta works (A II. 60, 61), which well repay a visit. They were built inside the farm buildings and many of the old bricks can still be seen embedded in the concrete. On the north-western outskirts of St. Julien is a long massive shelter, a former German Headquarters (A II. 62). It is situated about 100 yards off the Track leading from St. Julien to Alberta. In front on the west side of the road is Cheddar Villa (A II. 1) and on the east side about one-third of the way to Cheddar Villa is Van Heule Farm.

Mousetrap Farm, where the German gas attack was held up on the 22nd April, 1915, is on the ridge beyond and to the right of Cheddar Villa.

Farther down on the east side of the road the concrete shelters and emplacements near Wieltje and Pickelhaube

THE PILL-BOXES OF FLANDERS

House can just be distinguished. These are shown on the map as A III. 1–36, and deserve a close inspection. A III. 1–28, 30, 31, were known as Cambrai Trench and Cambrai Lane. Those to the north of the road (A III. 29, 32–36) were known as Call Trench and Call Support. Cambrai Trench was the actual German front line, and the concrete works in this locality were part of the first line system. The one-man machine-gun emplacements (A III. 27 and A III. 28) are of interest.

The groups of pill-boxes (A II., A III., B II.) give an excellent idea of the layout of the German defences in this sector. The front system at Wieltje comprised three or four successive lines of trenches with concrete shelters and emplacements. Then came the second line in front of St. Julien with its double line of trenches where the concrete dug-outs were almost continuous, and in rear a succession of strong points or defended localities such as Alberta, Maison du Hibou, Triangle Farm. All these blockhouses and trenches were mutually supporting, being located so as to protect each other by means of enfilade and oblique fire. Moreover, so skilfully were they sited that, previous to the 31st July, 1917, the opening day of the Battles of Ypres, 1917, the existence of a very large number of them was unknown to our troops, and so they were not affected by the preliminary bombardment.

It should be noted that, when the crops are fully grown, it is not always possible to locate certain of the pill-boxes and other points of interest from the position referred to above.

St. Julien. The first Gas attack.

No history of St. Julien would be complete without a reference to the events of 22nd April, 1915, when poison gas was used for the first time by the Germans.

At the beginning of April, 1915, the British front was extended from the Ypres–Menin Road to the Ypres–Poelcapelle Road. The Canadians took over the left sector (15th–17th April), and St. Julien was on the Franco-British boundary but inclusive to the British. The 3rd Canadian Brigade held the line of the Stroombeck, north-east of St. Julien. The 22nd April was a particularly beautiful spring day, but about 5 p.m. its quietude was ruthlessly disturbed by a terrific burst of heavy howitzer fire. Following this greenish-yellow clouds were observed rolling down towards the sector held by the French troops. Presently Algerians and French Territorials were seen hurriedly

THE PILL-BOXES OF FLANDERS

retreating and teams and wagons of French artillery moving to the rear. Terrified men passed by, coughing and pointing to their throats. The retreat was rapidly degenerating into a rout. By 7 p.m. the French guns were silent. The poison gas attack had succeeded and a great gap occurred on the Canadian left. On their immediate left some Tirailleurs and Zouaves held on, but all the Territorials and Algerians had disappeared and the German troops advanced, protected by a heavy barrage and machine-gun fire.

Two platoons of the 13th Canadians held the enemy at Mousetrap Farm (it can be seen, as one faces Ypres, to the right and beyond Cheddar Villa), fighting till every man was killed, whilst a Company of the 14th Canadians put up a stout defence at Hampshire Farm. For a time the left flank of the British Expeditionary Force ended abruptly just west of St. Julien, and from this point there was an undefended gap of $4\frac{1}{2}$ miles up to Brielen (on the west side of the Canal).

At 9 p.m. the Germans attacked the Tirailleurs on the Poelcapelle Road, but with the help of the 13th Canadians their advance was temporarily checked. The situation was, however, still critical, so in response to a request for reinforcements a company of the 2nd Buffs arrived and succeeded in the nick of time in reoccupying the original line and securing the apex of the Salient. During the night there was a lull in the fighting and the British gained time to push their few available reserves into the breach.

Battles of Ypres, 1917, 31st July-10th November.

It was, however, during the Battles of Ypres, 1917, that the pill-boxes in this area played such an important part. Before the first attack the British front line in this sector ran from a point on the Ypres–Zonnebeke Road, some 500 yards west of Verlorenhoek, thence to Warwick Farm, Wieltje, Cross Roads Farm, Turco Farm, Glimpse Cottage to the Canal about $\frac{1}{2}$ mile south-east of Boesinghe (*see* Map).

The battle commenced at 3.50 a.m. on the 31st July, 1917, having been preceded by a lengthy preliminary bombardment which, though it did cause some damage, was also unfortunately the means of completely disarranging the intricate drainage system in this part of Flanders. Added to this the weather, which up to 29th July had been fine, underwent a complete change. Heavy thunderstorms occurred which quickly turned the whole country, already churned up by the bombardment, into a sea of mud. When the actual attack

THE PILL-BOXES OF FLANDERS

commenced the rain held off, but low-lying clouds and threatening rain were evidence that the weather conditions would soon deteriorate. This was indeed the case, as shortly after 8 p.m. the rain came down steadily and remorselessly and continued with varying intensity for weeks. In fact, conditions could not have been worse. Shell-holes became feet deep in yellow slimy water. Mud changed from dough to slime. The whole surface of the ground consisted of nothing but a series of overlapping shell craters, through falling into which numbers of wounded and unwounded men lost their lives by drowning. Everything was discouraging and depressing enough to break the spirit of any but the British soldier.

The attack itself was delivered against an enemy whose fighting efficiency had by no means declined and whose numbers were still for all practical purposes undiminished. Further, the position to be assailed was hidden from view and had been deliberately fortified during the preceding two years. It contained numbers of concrete works constructed amidst the ruins of farms, concrete shelters and dug-outs, and many small forts or blockhouses, the existence of which had never been suspected. The British Infantryman went into action with the following equipment: Steel helmet, 120 rounds S.A.A. In his pack: towel and soap, oil tin, holdall, one iron ration and one day's preserved ration. He carried two water-bottles (one with cold tea), ground sheet, one rifle grenade, two flares, three sandbags, wire-cutters, entrenching tool, box respirator. Bombers carried eight grenades instead of the S.A.A. A heavy load under the most favourable conditions, but when account is taken of the terrain to be crossed it can only be described as overwhelming. The trenches from which the attack took place were merely breastworks with no cover from view and no view in front, in marked contrast to those held by the defence.

As the battle progressed all systems of communication, except runners, broke down. Visual signalling became impossible. Wires, when laid, were soon broken, and to make matters worse bad visibility caused all flying to be cancelled. Surely, never in history did men fight under more desperate conditions. As one well-known writer remarks: " Men who could continue for three months to attack under the conditions which characterised this most terrible battle of the war must indeed belong to an invincible stock."

THE PILL-BOXES OF FLANDERS

Wieltje.   A III. 1-36

The blockhouses and dug-outs opposite Wieltje (Cambrai Trench, Cambrai Lane, Call Trench and Call Support) were included in the sector of attack allotted to the 55th (West Lancashire) Division. This Division attacked with two Brigades (165th and 166th) in front and one Brigade (164th) in support. Cambrai and Call Trenches were taken by the 1/5th and 1/6th Battalions of the King's Regiment, the 1/5th King's Own and 1/5th Loyal North Lancashires, without a great deal of opposition except from flanking fire from various strong points on their right.

Pond Farm and vicinity.

The next objective was the system of trenches running from Spree Farm through Pond Farm (B III.) to St. Julien. Here severe opposition was met with, the enemy disputing the advance from every available position, particularly from   B III. these two farms and from Capricorn Trench, which ran parallel to and about 150 yards west of the road from Spree Farm to St. Julien. Spree Farm was eventually taken by a Battalion of the supporting Brigade (the 2/5th Lancashire Fusiliers) and was used as Battalion Headquarters for the rest of the day. Capricorn Trench fell to the Liverpool Scottish, 1/5th South Lancashires and 1/5th Loyal North Lancashires. But the losses of the Division were very heavy, one Battalion (the 2/5th Lancashire Fusiliers) had 473 casualties out of 593, and for some time was commanded by the Orderly room clerk. Pond Farm (B III. 1, 2)—a regular fortress—was for a short time in the hands of the 55th Division, but had to be evacuated owing to a heavy counter-attack which developed during the afternoon. It was never regained during the first phase of this battle. That this counter-attack did not penetrate farther was due to the gallant stand made by the Liverpool Irish (8th King's) and the 2/5th Lancashire Fusiliers, the remnants of which units were later withdrawn from action by a junior Subaltern of the Irish.

In the attack made by the 36th (Ulster) Division on the 16th August, a company of the Royal Irish Rifles surrounded Pond Farm on three sides, but owing to lack of supports it could not be carried and still remained in German hands. During the period 16th–20th August, it defied two further attempts at capture by troops from other Divisions. It was eventually and perhaps not inappropriately taken by the

THE PILL-BOXES OF FLANDERS

55th when this Division returned to the battlefield and renewed the advance on the 20th September. On this morning the line of Schuler Galleries fell to the Liverpool Irish and 2/5th Lancashire Fusiliers, the garrison of Schuler Farm capitulating to the former on the 21st September.

A II. 2–59, 60, 61 **St. Julien.** (*See Sketch A.*)

On the left of the 55th (West Lancashire) Division, the 39th Division attacked in the sector from the (inclusive) St. Julien Road to Kitchener's Wood. Canopus Trench (A II. 14–40) and the German second-line system here were taken by the 11th and 13th Battalions Royal Sussex Regiment, Canoe Trench (A II. 41–59) by the 17th Sherwood Foresters and 16th Rifle Brigade, and Canteen Trench (A II. 2–13 and 63–76) by the Royal Sussex with the help of the left Battalion of the 55th Division (The Liverpool Scottish). As was the case with the 55th Division, the first-line system was taken without difficulty, but the Canopus Trenches and the rest of the second line system proved a harder nut to crack, and it was only after a severe struggle that the Battalions mentioned above achieved their objectives.

Canteen and Canopus were held by the Sussex throughout the day, but at 6 p.m., owing to the heavy losses in these units and in other units of the 116th Brigade, the 16th Sherwood Foresters took over these two trenches with headquarters at Van Heule Farm. The strong points at Alberta (A II. 60–61) were a decided stumbling-block to the advance, but they were eventually captured by the 17th Sherwood Foresters. A passing tank was hailed and it succeeded in rolling a path through the barbed wire over which the Infantry assaulted under cover of a barrage from the 117th Trench Mortar Battery. One of the blockhouses was then used as a Brigade Forward Observation Post. The 1/6th Cheshires captured the outskirts of St. Julien, but opposite the centre of this village the 1/1st Hertfordshires suffered such severe losses as to be almost wiped out. The casualties of the 39th Division on this day amounted to 145 officers and 3,716 other ranks killed, wounded and missing. The 4/5th Black Watch when it came out of the line on 6th August was reduced to a mere handful, one company having only one officer and six men left !

B I. 3, 4, 5, 6, 7, 8, 9, 10 **Gournier Farm and vicinity.** (*See Sketch B.*)

On the left of the 39th Division, the 51st (Highland) Division attacked between Kitchener's Wood and Rudolph

German Concrete Blockhouse at Alberta, near St. Julien (A II. 60)

Copyright Imperial War Museum

[*Photo supplied by the Editor, "The Emblem"*
Old British Observation Post, Hussar Farm, Potijze

THE PILL-BOXES OF FLANDERS

Farm. This Division found the first line system of trenches badly damaged by shellfire and not held in any strength, so that no difficulty was experienced in its capture. The next system, however, being composed of the fortified farms and concrete blockhouses, was held in greater strength and proved a far more formidable obstacle. Amongst these were Gournier Farm (B I. 3, 4). The garrison of this farm had caused considerable casualties to the 6th Black Watch whilst waiting for the barrage to move forward. Accordingly, when the barrage did lift an attack was at once made on the farm. By working from shell-hole to shell-hole a platoon of this Battalion rounded it up, taking two machine-guns, twenty prisoners and a field gun. The Battalion, then, in conjunction with men of the 5th Gordons and a platoon of the 15th Welch Regiment, captured the blockhouses at Rudolph Farm and François Farm.

Grune Farm (B I. 8, 9, 10) and MacDonald's Wood were the scenes of severe fighting. MacDonald's Wood no longer exists, but its former position is immediately to the north of and adjoining Grune Farm. Two platoons of the 6th Seaforths attacked the farm, whilst platoons of the 6th Gordons joined in the fight and engaged the enemy in MacDonald's Wood. In addition, Tank G 50 appeared on the scene and shelled the farm. Eventually the Germans surrendered, ten prisoners being taken, together with a 4·2-inch howitzer and two machine-guns. The 6th Seaforths also captured Canister Trench. This trench ran from Gournier Farm in a north-easterly direction, and then round to the south edge of MacDonald's Wood. Two concrete dug-outs (B I. 4, 5) mark the site of this trench.

Iron Cross near Pilckem. (*See Sketch B.*)   B I. 1, 2

The blockhouses (B I. 1, 2) at Iron Cross were in the sector allotted for the attack of the 38th Welsh Division. Amongst their opponents was the Guard Fusilier Regiment (the famous Berlin " Cockchafers "). This regiment held their portion of the sector in depth, utilising all three battalions. They had only been two days in the line and were therefore quite fresh, but they were unable to offer an effective resistance to the Welsh attack. Of the 630 prisoners taken by the Division 500 were " Cockchafers." Near Iron Cross was a German telephone exchange and regimental headquarters where many prisoners were taken. The blockhouses (B I. 1, 2) were strongly held and the 14th Welch Regiment suffered many casualties before they effected their capture, 40 prisoners and two machine-guns being taken.

From the concrete blockhouse (B I. 1) a good view of the ground over which the Welsh Division advanced can be obtained, and to the south can be seen the farms (Gournier, Rudolph, François) referred to above.

The advance of the Welsh Division was then continued up to the Steenbeck. In spite of considerable opposition from machine-guns, firing from concrete emplacements inside the houses, all these strong points were outflanked and the garrisons compelled to surrender, the Steenbeck being reached and parties sent forward to hold and cover the crossings.

Many deeds of the greatest gallantry were performed by individual officers and men on that fateful day (31st July, 1917), and amongst them may be mentioned Captain N. G. Chavasse, V.C., M.C., R.A.M.C. This officer, whilst carrying a wounded man to his dressing station early on the 31st July, 1917, was himself severely wounded on the right side of the head. He still insisted on carrying out his duties and did not confine his work to those men who were brought to the dressing station he had established in the captured trenches. Repeatedly he went out with stretcher parties to the firing line in search of wounded, and to dress the wounds of those who were lying out. He insisted on carrying in under heavy fire a number of badly wounded men who were found in the open. Though suffering intense pain he continued for two days to attend to casualties, and during this time he had no rest.

At last, on the morning of the 2nd August, a shell pitched right into the dressing station and he received a terrible wound in the body. He was taken at once to the hospital at Brandhoek, but his case was hopeless and he died on the 4th August. His bravery was not of the reckless or flamboyant type, but the far finer bravery that sprang from his determination that nothing should stand in the way of whatever he considered his duty.

He had already received the V.C. in 1916, and for his wonderful conduct on this occasion he was awarded a bar to this decoration, being the sole individual to obtain this unique distinction during the Great War. It was indeed unfortunate that he never lived to receive this last award.

A II. 1 **Cheddar Villa.** (*See Sketch A.*)

Cheddar Villa (A II. 1)—a large concrete work, still in a fair state of preservation—was made considerable use of by

THE PILL-BOXES OF FLANDERS

British troops after its capture on the 31st July, 1917. It became a regimental aid post and subsequently a battalion headquarters (1/4th Oxfordshire and Buckinghamshire Light Infantry). Its situation, on the crest of a ridge, permitted of a very fair view of the surrounding country, but, as was the case with so many of the German blockhouses, it had a particularly wide entrance which, when in British hands, was completely exposed to enemy shells. On the night of the 7th-8th August, 1917, a platoon of the 1st Buckinghamshire Battalion was sheltering inside the opening trying to obtain much needed rest. The very first shell, which landed near the blockhouse, burst in the midst of the slumbering platoon. The effect was disastrous. Many were killed, and of those who were not killed several lost limbs. Fortunately one of the few who escaped was the Regimental Medical Officer.

Van Heule Farm was used as headquarters by the 13th Battalion Royal Sussex Regiment on the 31st July and subsequently by the 16th Sherwood Foresters. It was an unlucky choice, as a single H.V. shell caused over 30 casualties at this spot.

Triangle Farm and Maison du Hibou. (*See Sketch A.*)   B II. 1-4

These blockhouses are of great interest from a tank point of view. They are situated in the fields between Triangle Farm and Maison du Hibou and just south of the site formerly occupied by the redoubtable Cockcroft, which in 1917 was a regular fortress.

All these works were almost impervious to shellfire, had strong garrisons of machine-gunners and were surrounded by a mass of barbed wire. Between the 16th and 19th August, 1917, they had defied every attempt at capture, the Maison du Hibou blockhouses (B II. 2, 3) in particular having withstood two successive assaults delivered with the utmost gallantry by the 1/7th Worcestershires. On the 19th August the attack was renewed with tanks, eight being detailed for this operation. They advanced behind an artillery smoke barrage along the road leading north from St. Julien. As each tank came opposite its objective it left the *pavé*, plunged into the mud and struggled through the bog as far as it could go before sticking fast. The tank detailed for the Cockcroft got within 50 yards of its objective. The garrison, amazed at the appearance of this colossal engine of war, fled almost at once and the infantry platoon following occupied it without a casualty.

THE PILL-BOXES OF FLANDERS

The Maison du Hibou blockhouses were some way off the road, but the two tanks allotted for their capture managed to train a gun on the entrances, fired forty rounds at them and drove the garrison out.

The Triangle Farm blockhouses (B II. 1, 4) put up the strongest resistance, but with a tank in support were captured by " B " Company of the 1/8th Worcestershires (48th Division) in a hand-to-hand bayonet struggle. These successes were attained with the loss of only 15 men wounded in the infantry, whilst the tanks had only 2 killed and 12 wounded.

This affair is of particular interest as being the first definite success gained by the use of tanks in the 1917 offensives. Those who disbelieved in their use were silenced and the way was paved for the great tank attack at Cambrai in the following November.

26th JUNE, 1917

3rd SEPTEMBER, 1917

[*Copyright—Imperial War Museum*]

Air photographs showing ground north-west of Frezenberg, before and after bombardment

British Dug-outs at Lankhof Farm (A VI. 1-8)

Photo supplied by the Editor, "The Emblem."

THE PILL-BOXES OF FLANDERS

CHAPTER VI.
BORRY FARM, FREZENBERG. FITZCLARENCE FARM.

These works were in the sector of attack allotted to the **B IV. 1-10**
15th (Scottish) Division on the 31st July, 1917, and they were in the centre of a fierce struggle all through that day and again on the 1st August. Although desperate efforts were made to effect their capture, they still remained in German hands at the conclusion of the second day's fighting. On the evening of that day the 15th Division had succeeded in securing the line of the Frezenberg Ridge through Frost House, about 500 yards to the west of this line of blockhouses.

On the 16th August the attack was renewed by the 16th (Irish) Division, but little progress was possible owing to heavy fire from all the concrete blockhouses and emplacements in the vicinity, particularly from those at Borry Farm (B IV. 1—10).

On the 22nd August the 15th Division again attacked, Borry Farm being included amongst the objectives allotted to the 13th Royal Scots and 11th Argyll and Sutherland Highlanders, but so heavy was the enemy machine-gun fire that hardly any of the men of the leading companies survived. On the same evening a desperate effort was made by the 6th Camerons to take Borry Farm and Beck Farm, but without success.

On the 20th September the 9th (Scottish) Division was assigned the task of capturing this portion of the German defensive system, and finally Borry Farm and the concrete works to the south of it were taken by the 4th Regiment of the South African Brigade, which was at that time attached to the 9th Division. On this occasion a different plan of attack was adopted. The artillery put down a creeping barrage which gradually slowed down as the infantry advanced, and a proportion of smoke shell was allotted to all batteries. Instead of a succession of waves, the infantry attacked in lines of sections in file at 20 yards interval. To General Lord Horne should be ascribed the credit for introducing this new method of artillery support, which contributed so much to the success of this and subsequent operations.

Fitzclarence Farm. **B V. 1-2**

At Fitzclarence Farm, just south of Glencorse Wood, there are two concrete shelters (B V. 1, 2) which afford a good example of the skilful methods adopted by the German engineers in siting their defence works.

THE PILL-BOXES OF FLANDERS

CHAPTER VII.
THE AREA BETWEEN THE MENIN ROAD AND THE LILLE ROAD.

A IV. 1-10 **Greenjacket Ride.**

Just east of Sanctuary Wood and south of Stirling Castle are the pill-boxes along Greenjacket Ride (A IV. 1–10).

These mark the position of the old German Trenches known by our men as Jam Support, Jam Reserve, Jeffery Trench and Jeffery Support, and they formed part of the enemy first line defensive system.

They were included amongst the objectives of the 30th Division for the great attack of the 31st July, 1917, and were captured in the first rush by the 2nd Wiltshire Regiment of the 21st Infantry Brigade. This Battalion was one of the original units of the 7th Division, which played such a heroic part in the Battles of Ypres in October, 1914.

Bedford House.

Bedford House, the original name of which was the Château Rosenberg, was once a pleasant country residence. For some days during the Battles of Ypres, 1917, it was used as a Brigade Headquarters (the 55th), and throughout that period experienced the heaviest bombardment. It was many times hit by 8-inch projectiles, and in one day 500 gas shells descended in its neighbourhood. During the winter of 1917-1918 it was the headquarters of a 6-inch Howitzer Battery.

A V. 1-8 **Lankhof Farm.**

About ¼ mile beyond Bedford House is Lankhof Farm (A V. 1–8)—a collection of concrete shelters of British construction.

A VII. 1 **Battle Wood.**

At the south-west corner of the wood there is a massive dug-out built into a high bank on the west side of the road.

Page twenty-eight

THE PILL-BOXES OF FLANDERS

Gheluvelt. A VIII. 1

About 250 yards east of the crossroads in the village and on the south side of the Menin Road is a long concrete shelter which was used as the Headquarters of the German Heavy Artillery allotted to this sector of the defence. Many heavy batteries were located in the vicinity and four 8-inch howitzers were dug in immediately east and west of this shelter.

Gheluvelt will ever be associated with the name of the Worcestershire Regiment, for it was here, on the 31st October, 1914, that the 2nd Battalion, the last available reserve of the British defence, delivered the memorable counter-attack which resulted in the capture of the village and the closing of the gap in the British line which, had it been left, would have spelled almost certain disaster. Nearly four years later, on the 28th September, 1918, Gheluvelt was once more the objective of the Worcestershires. This time the 4th Battalion carried out the attack, moving up the Menin Road until it reached the rising ground at Inverness Copse where it deployed amidst drenching rain and advanced across the wilderness of shell holes which marked the site of Veldhoek. A battery of field guns was quickly overrun, and then through the falling rain came heavy bursts of machine-gun fire from the low ruins of buildings which loomed up alongside the road, and down the line ran the word that this was Gheluvelt. The pace increased, companies charged through the village and within ten minutes the ruins had been cleared and the Worcestershires were reassembling on the open slope beyond. They then captured the battery dug in alongside the road and the concrete dug-out at A. VIII 1, which was subsequently used as the Headquarters of the 88th Infantry Brigade.

This was the first day of the final advance on the Flanders front which resulted in the enemy evacuating Belgium and falling back to the Rhine.

THE PILL-BOXES OF FLANDERS

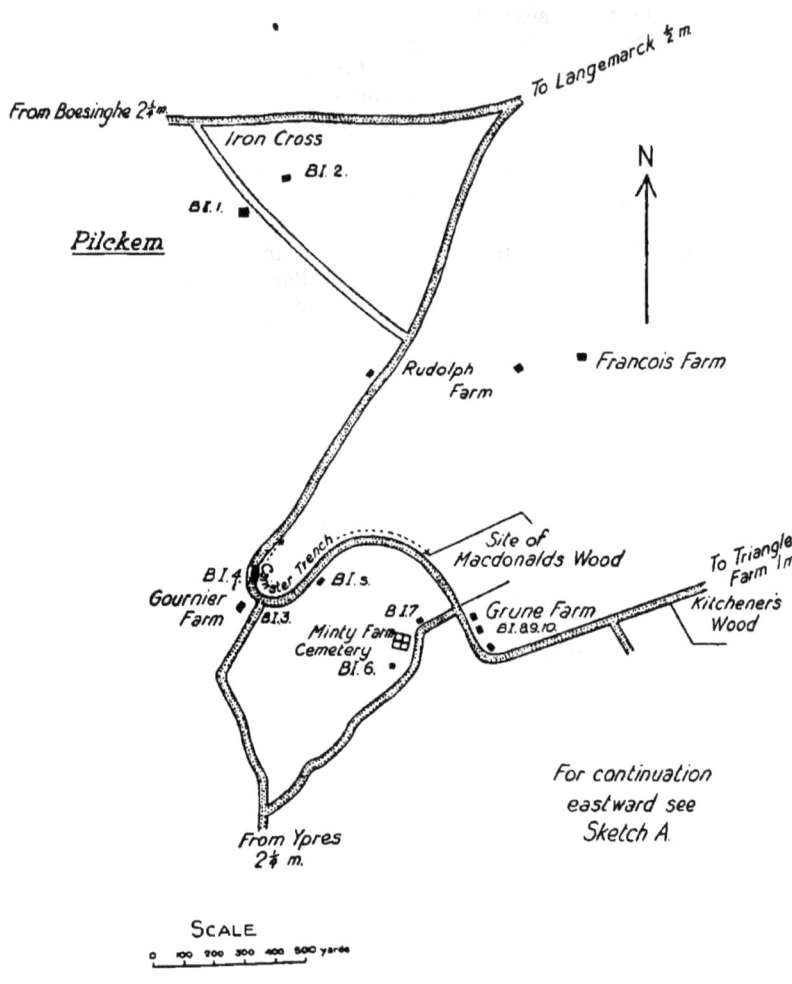

SKETCH B—Showing position of Pill-boxes in the vicinity of Pilckem
(*For continuation eastward see Sketch A*)

THE PILL-BOXES OF FLANDERS

CHAPTER VIII.

WYTSCHAETE-MESSINES AREA.

It is most unfortunate from the point of view of the A VI. 1-11, pilgrim and the military student that in this area, which B VI. 1-6 marked the scene of the most successful action in the whole series of trench warfare, nearly all the blockhouses and concrete shelters of historical interest have disappeared. The broken concrete has since been utilised to build up farm roads, re-lay courtyards, and generally assist in the programme of reconstruction. A few, however, do remain, and these give some idea of the layout of the powerful German defences. The attack on the Messines Ridge, which took place on 7th June, 1917, was one of the outstanding battles of the War. It was the first completely successful operation on the British front. It was the ideal example of the limited offensive. It was the most elaborate and carefully staged action ever fought by a British Army. The perfect liaison between all arms was a tribute to the excellence of the staff work. In all the initial stages of this operation every officer and man in the Second Army sensed the guiding hand of Lord Plumer, its Commander.

It is not intended to give a detailed account of the battle. To do so would take several chapters and there are many excellent accounts which can be studied. All that can be attempted here is to record briefly the historical incidents connected with the German works which to-day remain on the old battlefield.

The Divisions which took part in the main operation were the 16th, 19th and 36th of the Ninth Corps, the 23rd, 24th, 41st and 47th of the Tenth Corps, and the 25th, 3rd Australian, 4th Australian and New Zealand of the Second Anzac Corps, but it is on the front allotted to the 25th and 36th and, to a lesser extent, of the 16th, 19th and New Zealand Divisions where what remains of the German defensive works are to be found.

The extremely accurate shooting of the heavy batteries, which had faithfully dealt with all the enemy trenches during the seven days' preliminary bombardment, paved the way to success and incidentally was the means of saving

THE PILL-BOXES OF FLANDERS

hundreds of lives. As regards the wire cutting, on the Ninth Corps front alone there were 22,000 yards of wire, and the artillery task was to cut gaps 20 yards wide on every 100 yards of front. So successful were the results that no one was held up by wire and in many places the attacking infantry did not even have to lift their feet.

The battle started at 3.10 a.m.

The 3rd Australian Division and the New Zealand Division attacked on the right, the New Zealanders being on the left of the Australians. The principal objective of the New Zealand Division was the town of Messines. As was the case all along the front of the attack, no resistance was offered by the enemy in his forward or support trenches. Dazed and disorganised by the explosion of the mines and the terrific artillery fire, the few survivors surrendered, whilst the enemy barrage was unaccountably ragged and weak. In the path of the attack of the New Zealand Division lay the Moulin d'Hospice (A VI. 2). This was taken by the 1st Otago Regiment. Messines itself was literally packed with machine-guns and various close support weapons. In fact, it was a veritable fortress, but thanks to a carefully prearranged plan and the determination of the 4th Rifles and 2nd Canterbury Regiment, the enemy resistance broke down and the town passed into British hands after an interval of two years and eight months.

A VI. 1 Septième Barn (A VI. 1) was a strong point at the south end of a defended locality known as Owl Trench. The words Septième Borne (7th Km. Post) on a Belgian map had been transferred by a British map maker to a cottage close at hand in which the pill-box was constructed. It formed the objective of the 45th Australian Battalion. After severe fighting it was taken by two companies of this battalion on the afternoon of the 7th. But the enemy with little delay launched a powerful counter-attack and, owing to these two companies being isolated from the troops on their right and left, they were compelled to withdraw. At 8.30 a.m. the next day the same battalion again stormed and captured this section of the defences and, despite a bombardment which lasted for nine hours, succeeded in resisting all efforts of the Germans to retake it.

On the left of the New Zealanders the 25th Division advanced, their principal objective being the ridge between Messines and Four Huns Farm.

This Division had no less than nine distinct lines of enemy trenches to storm, but thanks to the excellence of the barrage

Page thirty-two

THE PILL-BOXES OF FLANDERS

and the fine fighting qualities of the infantry battalions concerned, the ridge was reached and secured in one hour and forty minutes, strictly in accordance with the time-table.

The blockhouses (at A VI. 4, 3) were taken in their stride by the 3rd Worcestershires and 10th Cheshires—Four Huns Farm on the Wytschaete-Messines Road by the 1st Wiltshires. A VI. 4, 3

Lumm Farm (A VI. 9), which was on the boundary line between the 25th and 36th Divisions, put up a stout resistance. The right company of the 15th Royal Irish Rifles met with very heavy machine-gun fire from this point, which temporarily checked their advance. The Company Commander thereupon ordered a platoon to attack it, supported by Lewis gun fire. The riflemen of this platoon worked their way up to the blockhouse and successfully bombed one of the chambers. In another the subaltern commanding the platoon had a hand-to-hand struggle with the German officer in command. The German gripped the Rifle officer round the waist, but he managed to get his arm free and put his opponent out of action. The men of the platoon then came tumbling down into the blockhouse and finished off the rest. About 15 prisoners were taken. The blockhouse itself is worth examining. It is some 200 yards from the main road and has several separate chambers. Subsequent to its capture it was used as a dressing station by an Australian Field Ambulance. A VI. 9

The 36th (Ulster) Division attacked on the left of the 25th, their principal objective being the summit of the ridge from Lumm Farm (A VI. 9) to the southern half of Wytschaete. The line of advance of this Division traversed the German front line system at a point known as the Spanbroek Salient. Under this Salient the 171st Tunnelling Company had driven a deep mine—one of nineteen that were constructed along the front of the attack. Up to the last minute it was doubtful whether this mine would go up, as the passage to the charge had been cut some time before by a German defensive "camouflet." On the eve of the battle the O.C. Company reported that the work was through and that it would almost certainly go up. As a matter of fact all nineteen mines were exploded simultaneously except the Spanbroekmolen which, however, was only 15 seconds late. So great was the noise produced by these explosions that it was distinctly heard in England.

The crater of the Spanbroekmolen mine still remains and will not be disturbed, as the site has been purchased by Lord Wakefield of Hythe. This mine was started on the

1st January, 1916, and completed on the 26th June of the same year. The length of the gallery was 1,710 feet and the depth of the charge below the surface of the ground was 88 feet. 91,000 lbs. of ammonal were used. The crater is 250 feet across and 40 feet in depth. On the north-west edge is a small concrete shelter (A VI. 5).

A VI. 5

As was the case with the 25th and New Zealand Divisions, there was no resistance in the enemy front and support trenches.

A VI. 6, 7 The blockhouses at A VI. 6, 7 were taken by men of the 9th and 14th Royal Irish Rifles, but the enemy put up a sturdy resistance in the next line of defence from the concrete works north of l'Enfer Wood, which housed German machine-gunners who fought, as always, with the utmost gallantry.

A VI. 8 Pick House (A VI. 8) was strongly held, but was eventually taken by the 10th Royal Irish Rifles, who used rifle grenades and a captured machine-gun with considerable effect. The garrison, which included a battalion commander, were all made prisoners.

By 8.40 a.m. on that day (June 7th) a line just west of the Wytschaete–Messines Road was being consolidated, some 2,500 yards from the starting point, whilst patrols were established 1,000 yards ahead.

The 16th (Irish) Division were on the left of the 36th, the northern half of the Wytschaete Ridge being captured by the 1st Royal Munster Fusiliers, who overcame the most determined resistance at this point. The next-door neighbours of the 16th Division—the 19th—had reached by 7.50 a.m. the St. Eloi–Wytschaete Road—strictly according to programme. Onraete Farm (A VI. 11) and Wood, which are referred to later, were taken by the 9th Cheshires.

A VI. 11

By the same hour the 7th South Lancashires had captured the blockhouse at B VI. 5 (Dome House), and by 10.15 the main chaussée Ypres–Lille had been reached. Oosttaverne Wood (B VI. 3, 4) was the prize of the 57th Infantry Brigade (8th North Staffordshires, 10th Royal Warwickshires, 8th Gloucestershires and 10th Worcestershires), which pressed forward with the utmost vigour and broke down all resistance at this point.

B VI. 5

B VI. 3, 4

The 41st Division took the Damstrasse, which runs in a north-easterly direction from Dome House (B VI. 5). This track is carried along an embankment for the first ¼ mile and is then continued through a deep cutting as far as the St. Eloi–Hollebeke Road. It is of interest as being almost the only area in the Ypres neighbourhood which retains traces of the

THE PILL-BOXES OF FLANDERS

old battlefields, no cultivation or afforestation having been attempted there. The blockhouse at B VI. 6 marks approximately the right limit of the attack of the 41st Division. B VI. 6

By the evening of the 7th all objectives had been gained, and the Second Army had advanced 1,500 yards beyond Messines and nearly 3,000 yards beyond Wytschaete.

The offensive was resumed on the 14th June, and amongst the objectives of the 25th Division was Deconinck Farm (B VI. 1, 2). For this operation battalions assembled in broad daylight, men being dribbled up in twos and threes behind the hedges. The significance of this movement was not detected by the enemy. The attack started at 7.30 p.m., and within 25 minutes all objectives were taken, Deconinck Farm falling into the hands of the 8th Border Regiment. B VI. 1, 2

Until April, 1918, the Messines Ridge remained in British hands, and during that period no specific action occurred on this front. But by the 6th of that month the German thrust directed on Amiens was stayed and Ludendorff, in order to retain the initiative, decided on an attack with limited objectives between the La Bassée Canal and Wytschaete. This he calculated would compel the Allies to absorb their reserves.

So on the 10th April the Fourth German Army, under cover of a thick mist and with a numerical superiority of 5 to 1, advanced and succeeded in overrunning the front and support line of posts (B VI., A VI. 1) held by the 57th Infantry Brigade of the 19th Division. By noon Messines had fallen and the enemy was close to the Wytschaete crest. Promptly a counter-attack was launched in which the 57th Infantry Brigade (8th Gloucestershires, 10th Worcestershires, 11th Royal Warwickshires), the 58th Infantry Brigade and the South African Brigade co-operated. Lumm Farm (A VI. 9) was again the scene of severe fighting and was eventually retaken by "D" Company of the 2nd South African Regiment. A VI. 9

Pick House (A VI. 8) was strongly held, and owing to the heavy losses already incurred the South Africans and the 58th Brigade were unable to recapture it. Messines, though penetrated, could not be retained, but the Moulin d'Hospice (A VI. 2) was held by the South Africans. A VI. 8

A VI. 2

For some 30 hours the enemy's advance in this sector was delayed, thanks to the tenacity, in face of superior numbers, of the South African and 57th Infantry Brigades. Eventually, however, as the result of the retirement farther south the line had to be withdrawn to the west of the Messines Ridge.

THE PILL-BOXES OF FLANDERS

A VI. 11
24th April,
1918.

Onraete Wood.

The ground surrounding Onraete Farm and Wood (A VI. 11) was on 24th April the scene of one of the most heroic episodes in the War. On that day the 1st East Yorkshire Regiment and the 1/6th West Yorkshires were holding from the south-east edge of the Grand Bois along the south of Onraete Wood as far as Zero Wood on the Wytschaete-St. Eloi Road. From 2.30 a.m. to 5 a.m. the Germans maintained a terrific bombardment on all the trenches and on all the avenues of communication. The whole area was drenched with gas. Every telephone wire was cut and even cables buried 8 feet deep were destroyed. Under cover of the smoke and a heavy mist, the enemy advanced, but the Yorkshiremen clung to the line and refused to give way. The headquarters of both battalions were completely isolated and the three front companies of the 1st East Yorkshires were surrounded and cut off. A sergeant of this battalion knelt on top of a pill-box and by rapid fire temporarily checked a hostile advance through a gap in the wire opposite the south end of Onraete Wood. The three leading companies of the West Yorkshires stood their ground and were all killed or wounded. The Company Commander of the support Company rallied his men from the top of a pill-box firing with his revolver till he fell severely wounded. Both battalion headquarters were annihilated, fighting to the last, and eventually only three officers and thirty other ranks of the East Yorkshires and a like number of West Yorkshiremen succeeded in withdrawing across the Wytschaetebeek. As the Brigade Diary briefly recorded : " They all fought at their posts and died there."

THE PILL-BOXES OF FLANDERS

CHAPTER IX.
1918—THE WITHDRAWAL IN THE SALIENT AND THE FINAL ADVANCE.

The ground gained in the Ypres Salient at such terrible cost was held throughout the winter of 1917-1918, but the German onslaught in the Somme area during March, 1918, and on the Lys in April of that year had compelled the British Armies in the south to give up an extensive area and in consequence a heart-breaking sacrifice had to be made. Owing to these untoward events it had become impossible to hold the line jutting out east of Ypres. To do so had always been a difficult task ; now it became a menace. So to keep the line intact and save Ypres a deliberate withdrawal was ordered, and all the ground that had been captured a few months before was yielded back to the enemy and a greatly restricted and far less vulnerable line was manned within a short distance of the ruined city.

Such was the situation in the Salient at the end of April, 1918, and no change occurred through the following three or four months. But during August and September the British Armies on the Arras and Somme fronts struck the first of their shattering blows that eventually broke down the German resistance. As the enemy was driven steadily backwards across the battlefield of France, his grip on the Ypres Salient gradually relaxed. He was forced to withdraw from the Kemmel area, and to take up a line which ran through Ploegsteert–Voormezeele and east of Ypres.

It was now the turn of the Belgian Army and the British Second Army in front of Ypres to attack, and operations commenced on the 28th September. The Belgian 8th Division advanced north of the Ypres–Zonnebeke Road, the Second Army to the south of that road, with the Second Corps (29th and 9th Divisions) on the left. Complete success attended the opening stages of this operation, and by the evening of the 28th September the British Second Corps held a line east of Gheluvelt–Becelaere–Broodseinde. Thus, in one day more ground had been gained than during the four months of terrible fighting in 1917 and the whole of the country which had been evacuated in the preceding April

THE PILL-BOXES OF FLANDERS

was now reoccupied. Rapid progress continued to be made, and by the 2nd October the Salient had ceased to exist.

* * * *

Such is briefly the story of these Flanders' pill-boxes. There can be no finer memorial to the indomitable spirit and magnificent fighting qualities of the British infantry soldier than these historic relics, and future generations may well marvel at the prowess and determination of those men who accomplished such feats of arms in effecting their capture. And to that gallant band who laid down their lives for their Country on this ghastly and terrible battlefield, no more fitting epitaph can be ascribed than those inspiring words of Laurence Binyon: "With proud thanksgiving let us remember our elder brethren. They shall grow not old as we that are left grow old. Age shall not weary them nor the years condemn. At the going down of the sun and in the morning we will remember them."

THE PILL-BOXES OF FLANDERS

ENVOI.

"Presently the order to 'march at ease' came down, and tongues were loosed. Someone in my Platoon began singing the verse of a song, and at the chorus the whole company joined in the swelling strain 'There's a long, long trail a-winding.' Even now, whenever I hear that wistful song, I can picture the Yeoman Rifles winding up that long, long trail; the Battalion at the flower of its strength, and the summit of its pride; for me, the mind picture I treasure most of all.

"Not so many miles away the guns were roaring, paving the way for the sacrifice which the Yeomen were to make a few short days hence. But here, in the quiet grey dawn, for me, the Battalion is still marching on till the day when I'll be going down the 'long, long trail' with those splendid souls who no longer march in the sight of men."

(From Sergeant Carmichael's Memories of the Yeoman Rifles (21st *King's Royal Rifles).)*
(Copyright reserved.)

APPENDIX

Key to Cemeteries Shown on 1/40,000 Map.

The Locations are given in Belgian Grid Co-ordinates.

Cemeteries marked thus * can only be approached on foot from the main road.

Cemetery Number		Co-ordinates East	North
58	Aeroplane Cemetery, Ypres	48·8—	172·6
7	Artillery Wood Cemetery, Boesinghe	44·7—	176·7
19	Bard Cottage Cemetery, Boesinghe	44·4—	174·2
93	Bedford House Cemetery, Zillebeke, Enc. No. 2	45·8—	168·7
91	Bedford House Cemetery, Zillebeke, Enc. No. 3	45·8—	168·9
92	Bedford House Cemetery, Enc. No. 4	45·9—	168·9
64	Belgian Battery Corner Cemetery, Ypres	43·8—	169·9
152	Berks Cemetery Extension (Hyde Park Corner), Ploegsteert	45·0—	158·7
149	Bethléem Farm East Cemetery, Messines	47·1—	161·2
148	Bethléem Farm West Cemetery, Messines	46·8—	160·9
73	Birr Cross Roads Cemetery, Zillebeke	48·6—	170·8
94	Blauwepoort Farm Cemetery, Zillebeke	47·1—	168·8
5	Bleuet Farm British Cemetery, Elverdinghe	41·9—	175·6
6	Boesinghe Churchyard	43·6—	176·3
38	Brandhoek Military Cemetery, Vlamertinghe	38·9—	171·6
36	Brandhoek New Military Cemetery, Vlamertinghe	38·6—	171·6
37	Brandhoek New M.C. No. 3, Vlamertinghe	38·7—	171·5
28	*Bridge House Cemetery, Langemarck	49·2—	174·4
26	Buffs Road Cemetery, St. Jean	47·7—	174·1
111	Bus House Cemetery, Voormezeele	45·6—	167·0
77	*The Buttes New B.C. Polygon Wood, Zonnebeke	52·9—	171·4
135	*Cabin Hill Cemetery, Wytschaete	46·7—	162·6
165	*Calvaire (Essex) Military Cemetery, Ploegsteert	46·2—	156·5
4	Canada Farm Cemetery, Elverdinghe	38·5—	175·5
10	Cement House Cemetery, Langemarck	47·4—	177·3
96	Chester Farm Cemetery, Zillebeke	46·7—	167·9
176	Cité Bonjean Military Cemetery, Armentières	43·5—	152·9
21	Colne Valley Cemetery, Boesinghe	45·1—	175·0
110	*Croonaert Chapel Cemetery, Wytschaete	44·6—	165·7
79	Dadizeele Communal Cemetery	59·8—	170·8
78	Dadizeele New British Cemetery	59·7—	170·8
126	*Derry House Cemetery No. 2, Wytschaete	46·4—	163·3
86	Dickebusch Churchyard	41·7—	167·8 N
88	Dickebusch New Military Cemetery	41·7—	167·8 S
89	Dickebusch New Military Cemetery Extension	41·7—	167·7
87	Dickebusch Old Military Cemetery	41·7—	167·8 Cen
63	Divisional Cemetery, Dickebusch Road, Vlamertinghe	43·6—	170·9
24	*Divisional Collecting Post Cemetery, St. Jean	46·4—	173·8
30	Dochy Farm New British Cemetery and Extension, Langemarck	51·8—	174·5

Page forty

THE PILL-BOXES OF FLANDERS

Cemetery Number	Cemetery	Co-ordinates East	North
9	*Dragoon Camp Cemetery, Boesinghe ...	45·4	176·3
137	Dranoutre Military Cemetery ...	37·9	162·0
44	Duhallow A.D.S. Cemetery, Ypres	45·0	173·1
97	*1/D.C.L.I. Cemetery, The Bluff, Zillebeke	47·5	167·9
16	Elverdinghe Churchyard ...	40·7	175·1
108	Elzenwalle Brasserie, Voormezeele	43·6	166·8
43	Essex Farm Cemetery, Boesinghe	44·8	173·5
177	Ferme Buterne Military Cemetery, Houplines ..	47·4	152·8
14	Ferme Olivier Cemetery, Elverdinghe ...	39·6	175·2
104	Godezonne Farm Cemetery, Kemmel	42·2	165·7
84	Grootebeek British Cemetery, Reninghelst	38·2	168·6
164	*Gunners' Farm Cemetery, Ploegsteert ...	46·1	156·6
13	Gwalia British Cemetery, Poperinghe	37·1	174·3
34	Hagle Dump Cemetery, Elverdinghe ...	38·2	172·5
98	*Hedge Row Trench Cemetery, Zillebeke	47·6	167·7
75	Hooge Crater Cemetery, Zillebeke	49·4	170·8
39	Hop Store Cemetery, Vlamertinghe ...	40·2	171·9
15	Hospital Farm Cemetery, Elverdinghe	39·4	173·6
173	Houplines Communal Cemetery Extension	47·4	153·4
85	The Huts Cemetery, Dickebusch	41·1	168·3
153	Hyde Park Corner (R. Berks) Cemetery, Ploegsteert ...	45·1	158·6
119	*Irish House Cemetery, Kemmel	43·1	163·9
141	Kandahar Farm Cemetery, Neuve-Eglise	42·6	160·6
116	Kemmel Château Military Cemetery ...	41·4	164·1
117	Kemmel Churchyard ...	41·5	164·2
106	Kemmel No. 1 French Cemetery	42·4	166·2
103	Klein Vierstraat British Cemetery, Kemmel	42·1	166·2
23	*La Belle Alliance Cemetery (Boesinghe)	46·2	173·8
47	La Brique Military Cemetery No. 1, St. Jean ...	46·2	172·8
46	La Brique Military Cemetery No. 2, St. Jean...	46·1	172·8
102	La Clytte Military Cemetery, Reninghelst	39·4	165·9
118	La Laiterie Military Cemetery, Kemmel	42·3	164·7
160	*Lancashire Cottage Cemetery, Ploegsteert	46·1	157·8
145	*La Plus Douve Farm Cemetery, Ploegsteert ...	43·8	160·4
100	*Larch Wood (Railway Cutting) Cemetery, Zillebeke ...	48·2	168·6
171	Le Bizet Cemetery, Armentières ...	45·7	154·1
168	Le Touquet Railway Crossing Cemetery, Ploegsteert ...	46·8	155·7
81	Lijssenthoek Military Cemetery, Poperinghe ...	32·5	169·1
127	Lindenhoek Châlet Military Cemetery, Kemmel	41·3	163·0
115	Locre Churchyard ...	37·4	163·8
121	Locre Hospice Cemetery ...	37·9	163·4
136	Locre No. 10 Cemetery ...	37·6	162·6
163	London Rifle Brigade Cemetery, Ploegsteert ...	45·0	156·8
132	*Lone Tree Cemetery, Spanbroekmolen, Wytschaete...	43·7	162·9
76	*Maple Copse Cemetery, Zillebeke	49·2	169·4
162	Maple Leaf Cemetery, Romarin, Neuve-Eglise...	41·9	157·1
68	Menin Road South Military Cemetery, Ypres...	46·9	171·2
134	Messines Ridge British Cemetery	45·8	161·7
11	Minty Farm Cemetery, St. Jean...	47·3	175·7
166	Motor Car Corner Cemetery, Ploegsteert	45·7	155·5
156	*Mud Corner Cemetery, Warneton	46·1	159·1
140	Neuve-Eglise Churchyard ...	41·1	159·7
8	New Irish Farm Cemetery, St. Jean	46·4	173·7
169	Nieppe Communal Cemetery ...	42·0	155·1

THE PILL-BOXES OF FLANDERS

Cemetery Number		Co-ordinates East North
32	Nine Elms British Cemetery, Poperinghe	32·4—171·5
22	*No Man's Cot, Boesinghe (51st Division Cemetery) ...	46·5—174·9
112	*Oak Dump Cemetery, Voormezeele ...	47·3—167·0
124	Oosttaverne Wood Cemetery, Wytschaete	46·6—164·9
56	Oxford Road Cemetery, Ypres ...	47·7—173·1
128	*Packhorse Farm Shrine Cemetery, Wulverghem	41·6—162·4
12	Passchendaele New British Cemetery ...	54·5—177·1
72	Perth (China Wall) Cemetery, Zillebeke	48·1—170·3
155	Ploegsteert Churchyard ...	44·8—157·3
159	*Ploegsteert Wood Cemetery, Warneton	45·8—158·1
3	Poelcappelle British Cemetery, Langemarck	51·7—178·8
59	*Polygon Wood Cemetery, Zonnebeke ...	53·0—171·9
129	*Pond Farm Cemetery, Wulverghem ...	42·5—162·2
161	Pont-d'Achelles Military Cemetery, Nieppe	40·5—156·2
170	Pont-de-Nieppe Communal Cemetery ...	43·0—154·7
33	Poperinghe Communal Cemetery ...	34·4—171·5
61	Poperinghe New Military Cemetery ...	34·7—171·0
60	Poperinghe Old Military Cemetery ...	34·5—171·4
52	Potijze Burial Ground, Ypres ...	47·4—172·2
57	Potijze Château Grounds Cemetery, Ypres	47·7—172·4
53	Potijze Château Lawn Cemetery, Ypres	47·6—172·4
54	Potijze Château Wood Cemetery, Ypres	47·5—172·4
147	*Prowse Point Military Cemetery, Warneton	46·2—159·3
42	Railway Château Cemetery, Vlamertinghe	43·6—171·4
69	Railway Dugouts Burial Ground (Transport Farm), Zillebeke ...	46·7—169·4
66	Ramparts Cemetery, Lille Gate, Ypres...	45·8—170·6
144	*Ration Farm (La Plus Douve) Annexe, Ploegsteert ...	43·8—160·6
35	Red Farm Cemetery, Vlamertinghe ...	38·2—171·9
83	Reninghelst Churchyard and Extension	36·9—167·6
82	Reninghelst New Military Cemetery ...	36·6—167·6
107	*Ridge Wood Military Cemetery, Voormezeele...	42·9—166·8
158	*Rifle House Cemetery, Ploegsteert Wood, Warneton ...	46·4—158·5
131	*R.E. Farm Cemetery, Wytschaete ...	43·5—162·0
74	R.E. Grave, Railway Wood, Zillebeke ...	49·2—171·3
2	Ruisseau Farm British Cemetery, Langemarck	46·7—178·4
45	St. Jan-ter-Biezen Communal Cemetery	30·1—172·3
48	St. Jean Churchyard ...	46·8—172·8
29	St. Julien Dressing Station Cemetery, Langemarck ...	49·1—175·3
143	St. Quentin Cabaret Military Cemetery, Ploegsteert ...	43·3—161·0
101	*Sanctuary Wood Cemetery, Zillebeke ...	49·1—169·1
27	Seaforth Cemetery, Cheddar Villa, Langemarck	48·6—174·4
17	Solferino Farm Cemetery, Brielen ...	42·8—174·2
122	Somer Farm Cemetery, Wytschaete ...	45·8—164·5
133	*Spanbroekmolen British Cemetery, Wytschaete	44·0—162·9
95	Spoilbank Cemetery, Zillebeke ...	46·4—167·8
154	Strand Cemetery, Ploegsteert ...	45·0—158·1
105	*Suffolk Cemetery, Kemmel ...	42·5—166·0
18	*Talana Farm Cemetery, Boesinghe ...	43·9—174·9
167	Tancrez Farm Cemetery, Ploegsteert ...	46·4—155·6
70	Tuileries Cemetery, Zillebeke ...	47·9—169·5
157	*Toronto Avenue Cemetery, Warneton ...	46·4—159·0
125	*Torreken Farm No. 1, Wytschaete ...	45·9—163·9

Page forty-two

THE PILL-BOXES OF FLANDERS

Cemetery Number		Co-ordinates East—North
25	*Track " X " Cemetery, St. Jean	47·5—174·3
31	Tyne Cot Cemetery, Passchendaele	53·8—175·0
151	Underhill Farm Cemetery, Ploegsteert	44·2—159·1
40	Vlamertinghe Military Cemetery	41·0—171·9
62	Vlamertinghe New Military Cemetery	40·9—171·0
90	Voormezeele Enclosure No. 1 / Voormezeele Enclosure No. 2 (Two separate adjoining Cemeteries.)	44·6—167·6
109	Voormezeele Enclosure No. 3	44·6—167·3
20	*Welsh Cemetery (Cæsar's Nose), Boesinghe	45·4—175·3
139	Wervicq Communal Cemetery	55·7—163·2
150	Westhof Farm Cemetery, Neuve-Eglise	39·6—158·7
67	Westoutre British Cemetery	35·6—165·8
80	Westoutre Churchyard and Extension	35·7—165·5
49	White House Cemetery, St. Jean	46·5—172·4
55	Wieltje Farm Cemetery, St. Jean	47·4—173·2
99	*Woods Cemetery, Zillebeke	47·7—167·9
142	Wulverghem Churchyard	43·1—161·1
130	Wulverghem-Lindenhoek Road Military Cemetery	42·4—161·6
120	Wytschaete Military Cemetery	44·8—164·0
45	Ypres Reservoir Cemetery	45·0—171·5
51	Ypres Town Cemetery, Menin Gate	46·4—171·5
50	Ypres Town Cemetery Extension, Menin Gate	46·4—171·6
113	Zandvoorde Churchyard	52·1—166·9
114	Zandvoorde British Cemetery	52·4—166·9
71	Zillebeke Churchyard	48·2—169.5

THE PILL-BOXES OF FLANDERS

INDEX

	PAGE
ADVANCE, Final, in the Salient	37
ALBERTA	12, 17, 18, 22
ALGERIANS	18
ARGYLL & SUTHERLAND HIGHLANDERS, 11th Bn.	27
ARTILLERY SUPPORT, New method of	27
AUSTRALIAN Battalion, 45th	32
AUSTRALIAN Field Ambulance	33
BATTLE WOOD	28
BECK FARM	27
BEDFORD HOUSE (Château Rosenberg)	14, 28
BELGIAN 8th Division	37
BELGIAN GOVERNMENT, concurrence in preservation of Pill-boxes	7
BLACK WATCH, 4th/5th Bn.	22
,, 6th Bn.	23
BORDER REGT., 8th Bn.	35
BORRY FARM	14, 27
BRIELEN	19
BRITISH LEGION, Efforts of, to preserve Pill-boxes	7, 9
BUFFS, 2nd Bn.	19
CALL SUPPORT	18, 21
CALL TRENCH	12, 18, 21
CAMBRAI LANE	18, 21
CAMBRAI TRENCH	12, 18, 21
CAMERON HIGHLANDERS, 6th Bn.	27
CANADIANS, 3rd Bde.	18
,, 13th Bn.	19
,, 14th Bn.	19
CANISTER TRENCH	13, 23
CANOE TRENCH	17, 22
CANOPUS TRENCH	12, 17, 22
CANTEEN TRENCH	17, 22
CANTERBURY REGT., 2nd	32
CAPRICORN TRENCH	21
CARMICHAEL, Sgt., Yeoman Rifles, Envoi by	39
CEMETERIES	7
CHÂTEAU ROSENBERG (see Bedford House).	
CHAVASSE, Capt., N.G., V.C., R.A.M.C.	24
CHEDDAR VILLA	17, 24
CHESHIRE REGT., 1st/6th Bn.	22
,, 9th Bn.	34
,, 10th Bn.	33
COCKCHAFERS, The Guard Fusilier Regt.	23
COCKCROFT	25
DAMSTRASSE	34
DECONINCK FARM	14, 35
DIVISIONS—	
9th (Scottish)	27, 37
15th (Scottish)	27
16th (Irish)	27, 31, 34
19th	31, 34
25th	31, 32, 33
29th	37

Page forty-four

THE PILL-BOXES OF FLANDERS

	PAGE
DIVISIONS—	
30th	28
36th (Ulster)	21, 31, 33
38th (Welsh)	15, 23, 24
39th	22
41st	31, 34
51st (Highland)	15, 22
55th (West Lancashire)	21, 22
3rd Australian	31, 32
4th Australian	31
New Zealand	31, 32
DOME HOUSE	34
DRAINAGE SYSTEM, in Flanders	19
EAST YORKSHIRE REGT., 1st Bn.	36
EQUIPMENT of British Infantryman going into action	20
ESSEX FARM	13, 15
FITZCLARENCE FARM	14, 27
FOUR HUNS FARM	32, 33
FRANCOIS FARM	23
FREZENBERG	14, 27
GAS, first use of by Germans, 1915	18
GHELUVELT	14, 29
GLOUCESTERSHIRE REGT., 8th Bn.	34, 35
GORDON HIGHLANDERS, 5th Bn.	23
,, ,, 6th Bn.	23
GOURNIER FARM	13, 22, 23
GREENJACKET RIDE	28
GRUNE FARM	13, 23
GUARD FUSILIER REGT., "Cockchafers"	23
HAMPSHIRE FARM	19
HERTFORDSHIRE REGT., 1st/1st Bn.	22
HORNE, LORD	27
HUSSAR FARM	14, 15
IMPERIAL WAR GRAVES COMMISSION, care of Cemeteries in Salient	7
IRON CROSS, near Pilckem	13, 23
JAM RESERVE	28
JAM SUPPORT	28
JEFFERY SUPPORT	28
JEFFERY TRENCH	28
JULIET FARM	17
KING'S OWN REGT., 1st/5th Bn.	21
KING'S REGT., 1st/5th and 1st/6th Bns.	21
KITCHENER'S WOOD	13, 17, 22
LANCASHIRE FUSILIERS, 2nd/5th Bn.	21, 22
LANKHOF FARM	14, 28
LIVERPOOL IRISH	21, 22
LIVERPOOL SCOTTISH	21, 22
LONE TREE CEMETERY	14
LONE TREE CRATER (Spanbroekmolen)	14
LOYAL NORTH LANCASHIRE REGT., 1st/5th Bn.	21
LUMM FARM	14, 33, 35
MACDONALD'S WOOD	13, 23
MAISON DU HIBOU	14, 18, 25, 26
"MEBU"	11, 12

Page forty-five

THE PILL-BOXES OF FLANDERS

	PAGE
MENIN GATE, Sounding of Last Post	7
MESSINES	10, 14, 32, 35
MESSINES RIDGE	7, 31, 35
MINES, Battle of Messines, 1917	33, 34
MINTY FARM CEMETERY	13
MOULIN D'HOSPICE	32, 35
MOUSETRAP FARM	10, 17, 19
NEW ZEALAND RIFLE BRIGADE, 4th Bn.	32
NOMENCLATURE of places in Ypres Salient, origin of	10
NORTH STAFFORDSHIRE REGT., 8th Bn.	34
ONRAETE FARM	34, 36
ONRAETE WOOD	34, 36
OOSTTAVERNE	14
OOSTTAVERNE WOOD	34
OTAGO REGT., 1st	32
OWL TRENCH	32
OXFORDSHIRE & BUCKINGHAMSHIRE L.I., 1st/4th Bn.	25
,, ,, 1st Buckinghamshire Bn.	25
PASSCHENDAELE	3
PICK HOUSE	34, 35
PICKELHAUBE HOUSE	17
PILCKEM	13, 23
PILLBOXES, Capture of, by individuals	12
,, Construction of	11
PLUMER, F.M., LORD	8, 31
POND FARM	13, 21
RIFLE BRIGADE, 16th Bn.	22
ROSENBERG CHÂTEAU (see Bedford House).	
ROYAL ENGINEERS, 171st Tunnelling Co.	33
ROYAL IRISH RIFLES	21
,, ,, 9th Bn.	34
,, ,, 10th Bn.	34
,, ,, 14th Bn.	34
,, ,, 15th Bn.	33
ROYAL MUNSTER FUSILIERS, 1st Bn.	34
ROYAL SCOTS, 13th Bn.	27
ROYAL SUSSEX REGT., 11th Bn.	22
,, ,, 13th Bn.	22, 25
ROYAL WARWICKSHIRE REGT., 10th Bn.	34
,, ,, 11th Bn.	35
RUDOLPH FARM	22, 23
ST. JULIEN	10, 12, 13, 17, 18, 19, 21, 22, 25
SANCTUARY WOOD	14, 28
SCHULER FARM	22
SCHULER GALLERIES	22
SEAFORTH HIGHLANDERS, 6th Bn.	23
SEPTIÈME BARN, also Septième Borne, origin of name	32
SHERWOOD FORESTERS, 16th Bn.	22, 25
,, ,, 17th Bn.	22
SOUTH AFRICAN INFANTRY, 2nd Bn.	35
,, ,, 4th Bn.	27
SOUTH LANCASHIRE REGT. 1st/5th Bn.	21
,, ,, 7th Bn.	34
SPANBROEKMOLEN CRATER	14, 33
SPANBROEK SALIENT	33
SPREE FARM	21

Page forty-six

THE PILL-BOXES OF FLANDERS

		PAGE
STEENBECK	...	24
STROOMBECK	...	18
TALBOT HOUSE, Poperinghe	...	3
TANKS	...	23, 25, 26
TERRITORIALS, French	...	18
TIRAILLEURS	...	19
TOC H, Efforts of, to preserve Pill-boxes	...	7, 9
TRENCH MORTAR BATTERY, 117th	...	22
TRIANGLE FARM	...	14, 18, 25, 26
VAN HEULE FARM	...	17, 22, 25
WAKEFIELD, Lord, of Hythe	...	33
WELCH REGT., 14th Bn.	...	23
,, 15th Bn.	...	23
WEST YORKSHIRE REGT., 1st/6th Bn.	...	36
WIELTJE	...	10, 13, 17, 18, 21
WILTSHIRE REGT., 1st Bn.	...	33
,, 2nd Bn.	...	28
WIRE CUTTING, by Heavy Batteries, in attack on Messines Ridge	...	32
WORCESTERSHIRE REGT., 2nd Bn.	...	29
,, ,, 3rd Bn.	...	33
,, ,, 4th Bn.	...	29
,, ,, 1st/7th Bn.	...	25
,, ,, 1st/8th Bn.	...	26
,, ,, 10th Bn.	...	34, 35
WYTSCHAETE	...	14, 31, 33, 35
ZOUAVES	...	19

www.ingramcontent.com/pod-product-compliance
Lightning Source LLC
Chambersburg PA
CBHW060222050426
42446CB00013B/3141